I KNOW TOMORROW

Poems

Riza Ramos

Cover photo of Saipan sunset
by: Ferdinand Ramos

Published and distributed by:
Riza Ramos Books
8323 SW 69th Place
Gainesville, Florida 32608

Educational institutions
government agencies
libraries and corporations
are invited to inquire about discounts.
Contact: rizaramospoems@gmail.com

Retail cost: $14.95
ISBN-13: 978-0982868447
Printed in the United States of America

Table of Contents

Poems About Hopes

ACKNOWLEDGEMENT

I am thankful to the editors of the two major English-language newspapers in Saipan in which some of these poems were first published. Thank you Zaldy Dandan of Marianas Variety and Jayvee Vallejera of the Saipan Tribune for your support.

I am grateful to author and coach, Walt F. J. Goodridge, for his encouragement and guidance throughout the process and, most of all, for believing in me.

I am thankful to my husband for driving me to all the coffee places I wanted to go to write, and for keeping up with my poetic and creative ways.

I am thankful also to the people who touched my emotions, and the places that inspired my poetic imagination — good or bad, I let it all bleed on paper.

Dedication

for my mother

Patrocenia

You must be proud
somewhere out there to see me
fulfill my dreams.

AUTHOR'S NOTE

When I was in high school, I joined a poetry writing contest; not because I wanted to, but because there was no representation for freshmen. I won. That was unexpected. That day I discovered something about myself: I am a poet! Yet I never really took it seriously.

In my senior year, poetry was taught with English Literature. I was given the assignment of writing a poem, and through this, my fascination with poetry was restarted. The rest, as they say, is history.

My college years were entirely different. As a nursing student, I wrote poems when my brain cells became exhausted from memorizing the musculoskeletal system of the human body, and often to break the ice in the middle of my final examination review.

Going through an emotional adulthood, I've found refuge in poetry. As an introvert, I am not comfortable sharing sensitive thoughts with family and friends. I pour them all into poetry: my hopes, my dreams, my joys, my pains, my frustrations, my sentiments, my anger and my love. Most pieces were originally written in a faded notebook I've kept in a bag out of sight.

In 2006, I was hired as a staff nurse by the Commonwealth Healthcare Corporation and moved from the Philippines to Saipan, Commonwealth of the Northern Mariana Islands. I started sharing my talent in the English-language newspapers. Becoming a "nurse poet" helped to balance my life.

Sometimes, when I come home from a hard day's work, I open my laptop and just start writing as a stress reliever. At times like these, my husband knows it's his turn to cook dinner!

By 2019, I felt I had all the poems I needed to make a book, but I had many excuses. Finally, in March 2022, I broke the curse of procrastination (I had COVID and I thought that was the end of my world) and made this poetry collection into a publication.

I Know Tomorrow is about the stages of my life journaled as poetry. For years, these poems comforted me in many ways, and now I am sharing these with you.

I hope this book will inspire dreamers like me, especially those who are impatient to achieve their goals. Furthermore, I wish that this book will be a source of strength for those who struggle, offer relief to worried hearts, and restore faith to those who need to know that things will get better tomorrow.

I dream what I want and do what I dream, hoping tomorrow they'll come true. Today is the tomorrow a few years back. But tomorrow seems like forever.

Poems
About
Dreams

Dreams

Dreams start to happen
when you envisioned them
dreams are the foundations
of ours tomorrow
and whatever life may seem
dream and the universe
will hear and listen
for nothing is more powerful
than dreams
dreams are the blueprints
of our future
the footprints of yesterday
that will leave some space
in our hearts and in our minds
and as long as the sun rises
tomorrow will be all right

Cascade

Never turn
just wait along
against the stream
of life's tune
dreaming the night away
chasing to foresee the glory
dreary hammock
waves caressing rocks
enormous world
aloof chances
shimmering gold
drastic changes
hopes to await in an array
tomorrow or might someday
cascade chances of glory
comes my way

Waiting for My Dreams

While waiting
I'll write some poetry
about a heart that loves unconditionally
I'll write some essays
about peace and human kindness

While waiting
I'll walk down to the beach
and watch the sun
as it slowly sets
to kiss the ocean

While waiting
I'll plant some trees
up on the hill
where the strong wind blows
the view's breathtaking

While waiting
I'll pray fervently
for prayers concede barriers
throw down walls
and move mountains

While waiting
I'll dance in the rain
sing on stormy nights
to ease some pains

While waiting
I'll continue to dream
for dreams won't stop in the rain
though the skies are filled with clouds
or when the days are dim

While waiting
I'll be hoping
for if I won't
then why am I waiting

Hold On

Hold on to that dream
like symphony
some music of yesteryears
still sweet to your ears
feel it
enjoy it
make it grow
like those gigantic trees
with arms dancing with pride
multiply it
as much as the sands on the shores
as much as the stars at night
hold it tight
never let it fleet

No Haste

Blue skies
birds fly
by the window
I could throw a glance
I can walk at my pace
of far or near distances
down the sea
foaming tides
roaring waves
divers glide
I want to make it
unto the peak
unto the zenith
of my dreams
so long
until the wait is over
but can't wait enough
to grasp the moon
to win that laugh

Derailed

I stepped on the platform
waiting for my train
there were dark skies
thunderstorms and heavy rain
I pulled my luggage
full of hopes and dreams
beside me was an old lady
gaunt and frail eyes deep-seated
she asked me where I'm going
I said for now I can't answer
I'll let this train
bring me somewhere
where the mountains are high
where the grass is green
or some places I've never been
in ten minutes the rushing train came
the train was late
but who's to blame
I sat beside the old lady
with no words uttered
then suddenly the train jerked
this is a minor problem
the conductor announced
at first
was a commotion
then things seemed in control

I decided to break my silence
to the old lady and said
this train might be derailed
but I could use another route
I could ride the plane
the bus or the boat
or I could take the road
with my own two feet
any ways that could bring me
to the place
I want to be

Just Wait

Don't rush
you might trip
don't haste
you could stumble
break or fall
take it slow
the universe always got something
to offer you
if today you don't know
tomorrow it unfolds
take your time
stop worrying
but dance
sing
glide
hop
swim
love
hate
cry
smile
dare to take the risk
the world is a huge space
to fill your dreams

Awaken

Painted photography
doodled imagery
in my mind
I've sketched the patterns
over the years
on the paper
on the sand
on the shore
I've drawn them all
on the water
on the wall
dreams may disappear
unto the clouds
unto the thin air
some dreams
I allowed to sink
into the oblivion
into the aisle
of the unknown
but dreams awaken
on its own
some signs I heed
got my arms widespread
ready to spearhead

No Dream Is Free

I dream because it's free
no it is not
I need to toil
harder and harder
beyond my comfort zones
beyond my imaginations

though the world is big
I got nothing to fear
though things happened
not the way I imagined
I am in control

amidst the hardships
consistency is the key
turning night into a day
who says to dream is free

night shift RN

Riza Ramos

In Search for My American Dream

I found a fork
in the middle of the road
and found myself confused
whether to go south
whether to head north
or go back to the coast

then I asked myself
where to find the spoon
It could be
in the middle of the road
somewhere in the county
somewhere in the city
somewhere in the mountains
somewhere in the plains

the spoon need not be silver
neither be gold
as long as it can fit
into my mouth
over a load of food

Allow Your Dreams to Take You

wherever you want to go
you don't resist you don't complain
that's how simple and plain
dreams have minds of own
dreams have forces unknown
they have timings not too late
or not too soon
but mostly
they come out of expectations

Riza Ramos

We'll Meet Someday

I took a rope
I made some loop
tied to the edge
of this old bridge
the other end
around my waist
something to grab
if the bridge breaks
how to get to
the other end
is to ditch fears

rickety and slippery
courage and bravery
anyhow anyway

will meet someday —
dreams

Whatever struggles we had, tomorrow is always there for a brand new start.

Poems
About
Struggles

Day Job

Life is not about wanting more
by depriving myself
what I really need
what I truly deserved
not too lavish just adequate

Yesterday I was about to buy some bread
but the bread cost seven dollars so I halted
I pondered
if I can give twenty dollars to some strangers
or send two hundred dollars
back home to the Philippines
but I can't buy myself some seven dollars bread
then something is wrong

I told myself
not to take any calls today
or pick any shift
I'd rather be at the beach
reading my favorite book
rocking my hammock
on days off

Writer's Block

Writer's block is daunting
I waited for the gods
but they never came
then I saw some broomstick
I used to drive some mice
in our garden
then a lightbulb appeared
in my mid forehead
I tried to be in the zone
gone were the days when
I am brimming with words
gone were the days when
I am showered with ideas
I think I need to
eat some pickles

An Old Familiar Tune

Please cast some light
upon the gloomy clouds
an old familiar song
beautiful as it sounds
through the years
same old promises
same old tune
but not for me alone

Words of assurances
words of broken promises
I must go out of the zone
of impending doom
I made my way out
I worked hard and proud

Assurances gave me hope
to go on each day
thoughts of those promises
made me strong and stay
how would I know if it's true
I'll just wait and see
I waited
and waited

Until one day I got so tired
I thought about it a hundred times
then I made my ways
from the beach
to the prairies

Stuck

For quite some time
I'd been stuck in your arms
for a while
your words
your promises
are my lamps
in a dark room
they gave me hopes
then one day I realized
I saw some signs
promises delayed
are promises broken
what we had
is not worth keeping

The Grind

Every day is
pushing through the limits
beating the odds
learning new lessons
forgetting the past
go with the flow
adopt with what's new
saving the old
doing as told
coping with change
dealing with ambiguities
falling in line
no time to whine
chasing the rush
taking it slow
or doing everything today
though there's still tomorrow

Me

It's me
behind others
a choice
not a chance
some good music
I need it
where I am
where I belong
where I'd been
there are flaws
anywhere it shows
no mountains
no walls
broken hearts
forgotten dreams
rainy days
it all may seem
from giving much
from being too kind
leaving myself behind
some reward
I need a break
sometimes
I ought to see the sun

I'd been chasing the rain
a whole lot
for quite some time
I need to laugh
that boisterous laugh
I deserved it
when nothing else matters
one thing does —
myself

Shoes

Wear my shoes
if you can walk a mile
I will applaud
I will smile
and
I will give you
the right
to criticize

Bend

You may see me cry
you may see me sigh
you may see me stumble
you may see me fall
like a sandcastle
too vulnerable
but I won't give up
though this life's tough
through my struggles
you may see me bend
but no I won't
I'll never break

Let It Rain

It feels good
to walk in the rain
rain hides those tears
to ease thy pains
stride
walk
like you don't know
where you're going
when the rain stopped
you realized
the rain brought you somewhere
your tears still shed
the rain still falls
unto your eyes
until the sun shines
but for now
let it rain

You Loved

Your dream as a child wasn't realized
you became someone else
and you learned to love what you do
you became good at it too
sometimes
you wished you were that someone else
you wished to be out there
somewhere
in a place where you could be
who you are
you changed yourself
to fit in
what you wanted to be
you forgotten
because
you are a mother of a child
you are a wife to a husband
you are a daughter of a mother
you are a sister of a brother
you are a bless
to someone else
you became heartless toward yourself
because you think of them first
you became numb
to every hardship you had
you are who you are
because you loved

Daisy Love
a poem for my mother

She sang old melodies
as she watered her daisies
aching back on her sixties
she found happiness
upon the beauty of her flowers
she watched her garden bloom
like some paintings' showrooms
she never felt tired
of tending to her garden wide
one day I went home
from my adventures
I saw her garden
dry leaves had fallen
some red roses survived
greeted me as I arrived
some days she was bitter
some days she was tough
most days she was loud
today every daisy that I see
reminds me of her love

Riza Ramos

Gaping Wound

She became bitter
and bitter every day
and I thought
the bitterness was
meant just for me
because I gave her some pain
but I never knew
she was broken
she was shattered
more from deep within
she tried to hide her tears
for years
and she was bleeding
to me
who didn't cause
much of her pain
and the wound
was deeper than I thought

Faces

When friends' faces
turns to masquerade
when friends cease
dancing songs you played
nothing stays the same
rules may change for an old game
but those true will remain
in changing times who's to blame
the gator
the duck
or the penguin
I got nothing to lose
I got nothing to gain
in thunder and storm
in sunshine or rain
those true friends shall remain
though nothing stays the same

Sticks and Bricks

There was an unknown gap
a barrier
which I didn't know
what made me distant
away from you
some silk membranes
I built for myself
unconsciously
to be selective
of whom to trust
of whom to believe
or who's allowed to enter
my circle of friends
I thought the barrier
was made of senseless cobwebs
built by circumstances
all along on your side
the barrier was made
out of sticks and bricks

Expectations

I admit
oftentimes I break
for expectations not meet
for those I helped
can't give back the favor
that they once received
when they're in dire need
but
I must realize
out there in the open
someone else is designed
to give what I need
because
people have different
roles they played

Spot

In our lives
we often take the road
frequently traveled
for we are afraid of change
but without change
we can't progress
if we avoid the battled highways
we missed out on opportunities
that lay past that fork in the road
sometimes the destination we had in mind
feels underwhelming
compared to the spot
found in the middle of nowhere

collaboration with Ford RN

I'm Not Like You

I'm sorry I'm not like you
or anyone else
I'm a unique being
of unique entities
I can't hit the tune
like the way you sing
I don't enjoy the dance floor
or the strobe lights swing
I'm sorry I'm not like you
neither like your friend
I can't cry more
for a broken heart to mend
I can't stride or run
as fast as you can
yeah we're all different
the creator got a plan
I'm sorry I'm not like you
neither like your mother
I fear cockroaches and ghost
and some days I'm bitter
I can't speak my mind
so boldly and bright
I can only mumble to myself
scribble stare and write

Riza Ramos

I'm sorry I'm not like you
that guitar I can't strum
I can't play the piano
I can't beat the drum
I'm sorry I'm not like you
so don't compare
don't expect don't judge
I have my part I have my share

Fought

In this tough world
the strongest survives
give some chance to
the vulnerable
not to fall
but to fight —
I will fight

Cast the First Stone

Blamed
for mistakes she did
condemned
for the sins she committed
judged
for her wrong deeds
like there's no space
for atonement

Butterfly in the Ship

From subconscious
some memories leaked
I haven't cried enough
the pain I allowed to sink
in my thoughts
for all those years
I repressed some tears

It feels like yesterday
when you were miles away
no one to comfort me
in my pain and misery
from Manila to Leyte
I embarked on a long trip
moments lost I allowed myself to slip
my tears fell as I climbed aboard
the foaming waves became a road
smaller and smaller
the tall buildings became smaller
as the ship swiftly roar
the port became further and further
until I didn't see any at all
but the clear blue skies
and the ocean's deep blue
the ship seemingly soared
my chest felt like choked

as I was about to cry
I saw a yellow butterfly
from deep sadness I closed my eyes
mother said,
"The butterfly kept kissing you
until you've fallen asleep"
but until now
I don't understand
how a butterfly boarded the ship

One Little Baby Step

She didn't know how to start
picking up the broken pieces
I knew how badly she was hurt
in her face I saw the emptiness

I knew how she fought
I saw her worn-out face
many things she thought
would give her so much grace

one little baby step at a time
she got up and moved forward
determined to make a brand-new start
though it still pains though it still hurts

Time Machine

You wished
you owned a time machine
when the sands of time
has stopped from falling
your world stopped revolving
alone with your pain

you need to close
that chapter of your book that hurts
because
there's a second part
to get over
there's a second part to heal
and though you don't need a time machine
time is a perfect healer

No Promises

Don't promise me
if you knew you will fail
just leave with no words
so I'll expect nothing

but you promised me instead
you'll be coming back to me
no matter what happens
or whatever our future brings

and the road lead us back together
may not be as smooth as it was
but it's the place we've been

If Only

In retrospect
I saw my younger self
some disbelief
a grief
troubled dreams
a mistake
I tried to make amends
then you redeemed
my solitude
if I could bring back yesterday
back where we used to be
I would do things as they say
but if I did
today
where would I be?
whom I am with?

Space

It's the white blank pages
in my computer
or the soft comfy couch
it doesn't matter where
it's the empty cupboard
or empty oven
no one really cares
or the vast distances
between the galaxies
from Mars to Earth
baby
it's how far you are from me

Waiting

Waiting
is the hardest part of the going
but it's a joy
to think that leaving
means someone is waiting
it isn't fair
for the ones being left
long-distance love
dare not to ask
it will break your heart

Afloat

Row your boat
keep it afloat
reach out
shout
make it loud
louder
cry
no one even cares why
tears sometimes
need to be dried
out of your eyes
dance
to any tune
you're not alone
sing
unfamiliar songs
have some fun
face your problem
don't turn don't run
be proud
of whatever you have
you toiled so hard
you deserved what you got

Riza Ramos

Tide

I let you come rushing
into my life
to bathe those pitted rocks
to sing a loud melody
when all that matters to me
is serenity
tide
I don't want you
swirling around my ocean bed
but without you
there's no beauty
you are my harmony
in my ocean's symphony
so let's dance
in my ocean's floor
tide
bring me some more

The Ship

Left the shore
steered my wheel
bound somewhere
my luggage
there's nothing in it
but loved ones' keepsakes
adrift
at first
in the oceans of dreams
I must
I will
bring this ship to moor
but never to drop the anchor
I'll brave the storm
and the coldness of the sea
for my dreams
will keep me warm
gigantic waves
I'll glide
through them
no
there's nothing to worry about
the stars are my guide
through this journey of mine
home is green father's word
but greener one if I could

Riza Ramos

If I stayed
and never pulled the anchor
what would I become
I will steer
through all kinds of water
or through thick and thin air
for I am a ship
and ship sails

inspired by migrant workers

Still

There were times
I wished to be
just in one place
in my comfort zones
and never leave
but I need to move
not for myself
but for the people I love most
I get by day to day
I surpassed all the pain
I kneeled and pray
that things will get better
someday
I fend for myself
you don't know
what took me to get through
or how long I endured
to be where I am now
to make ends meet
you don't know my plight
so don't envy
you have no right

Riza Ramos

Raindrops in My Eyes

In the apartment
where we moved
we slept on the floor
so chilly and cold
some bees invaded
the ceiling and front door
I woke up one night
with raindrops in my eyes
from the leaking tin roofs
I silently cried
in disbelief
looking at my children
I promised myself
to give them things
I never had as a child
I never slept on the floor
neither had a house with leaking roofs
nor broken doors

Paperboat

Wind whistling
glass breaking
people screaming
hearts pounding
pitched black night

daylight
flooded room
we emerged
from the bathroom
we hid from
the torrent storm
floor was flooded
I waded
then I smiled
a paper boat
touched my foot

typhoon Yutu Saipan 2018

Low Tide

It won't constantly happen
for the waves to be kissing the shore
the corals and rocks I've seen today
so much different than before
the sea bed wasn't made all out of the sand

and as the tide recedes
whatever
beneath the ocean floor
was revealed

Faux

Charmed by your magical words
I was tamed
total admiration
awe in my eyes was seen
years of magical feelings
what's missing was found
what comes from the heart was pure
what comes from the heart was profound

then our world turns bitter
which I never thought it would be
and I realized
that villains are clothed
most often
in lambskin

Pinch of Guilt

I felt some pinch of guilt
setting boundaries
pulling the hinges
of the strong bridge
that binds us
I'd rather be silent
keep the pain to myself
for you'll hate me
if I speak
when I am hurting

Bugs and Mugs

I don't fear anymore
I'd been waiting for this stage of life
to say this to me
growing up I feared a lot
not just with snakes and bugs
but with you who got mad
when I broke some mugs

I don't fear anymore
I never thought I can say this now
to do what I feel like doing
because I am allowed
or to love whom I think is lovable
and deserving of my love

I don't fear anymore
to make mistakes
or do whatever it takes
I am responsible
for the consequences
of every action that I make
It's the adult in me that's in control
because this child has grown

Overpowered

Kind deeds
big or small
you did for me
I remembered

Then one day
things changed
bright and sunny skies
were clouded

you broke my trust
then all those deeds —
big or small
I tend to forget

A Handful

I used to give
even the food that I must eat
then I started to realize
I am getting older
I must save for myself
a meager or a handful
something I never had before
I never saved
knowing I could be hungry
now I began
to think of me

inspired by the "Poor Dad Rich Dad" book
by Robert Kiyosaki and stories of migrant workers

A Gem

I want to throw to you
some rocks
I'd been keeping long
deep inside my heart

But
instead
I will polish them
and turn into
some precious gem

The Guest

She saw
the crowd of families
photographs perfect
tears trickled down her cheeks
disinvited
denied
disrespected
alienated

Pain Is Made Of

silence and fear
sadness and despair
what was left out of the pain
from deep within
soon
it will subside
sometimes all we need
is someone to apologize
but few will realize
what a broken heart really needs
for the time being
until catharsis feeds

Healing Quietly

You were silenced by the pain
then you decided to move on
though it wasn't easy
But you are a slow healer
no one can blame you
you are built that way

You grow every day
you heal every day
you heal quietly

Unsuppress

We should forgive
we should forget
all must be love
no time for hate

Yet
Is it fair for emotions to suppress?
Is life short enough to hold back
emotions while given the chance to live?

Anxiety

the curtain is slowly moving
away from the center
of the stage you are performing
revealing
unfolding
your heart beats so fast
like thunder rumbling
the audience are applauding
your act must be perfect
everyone is watching
you should perform as what
is expected as what they paid
and you perfectly nailed it
because you trust the process

New Venture

It's quite an adventure
to move
and follow some new path
or venture anew

what we left behind
somewhere
somehow
we'll be able to find

Do you want to know what hope means?
It's when I hear a child laughing
or see a child smiling.

Poems
About
Hopes

Sedated

Beautiful lights
I noticed that night
I was on a bus
that never stopped
it kept circling
it kept turning
back to where I've been
it was cold
the night seemed endless
some passengers get off
I kept still
I don't know where to go
the bus kept on returning
around where I've been
there were flickering lights
from the houses across the lake
visible steaming chimneys
and smokestacks of old factories
there was an old man
in front of my seat
I just enjoyed the ride
watched the spectacular northern lights
I slept
when I opened my eyes
everyone has left

"Where are you going?"
The bus conductor asked.
"Though this bus could take you
to anywhere you want to go
where you're going I must know!"
The bus conductor demanded.
"I don't have a destination in mind
so
wherever this bus may take me
I'll just enjoy the ride."
I insisted
I slept
The bus kept moving
back again to the place I'd been
I heard a baby crying
I opened my eyes
to the most beautiful sight —
a gift of life

My Inspiration

He brightens up the space
whenever he's around
he got round eyes
so much joy could be found

He fills the space
with much fun and cheer
he has beautiful smile
that made my gloomy days brighter

He fills my heart
with so many dreams
whenever I'm weary
he's my sugar and cream

He fills my heart
with much delight
and when he sings
I know the future
will be bright

Moments

I want to enjoy the moments
both happy and sad
the struggles and pains
all the emotions I have
for eventually
I will look back
to remember those moments
what matters most is
I enjoyed
every minute
and every second of it

I Know Tomorrow

I know tomorrow
even if I haven't been there
I don't own a magic
I'm not a fortune-teller

I got some secrets
with you I want to share
that I know tomorrow
even if I haven't been there

We worked and toiled
for our food tomorrow
we'd been told that
we reap what we sow

Looking back
if yesterday was gold
make today even better
then the future is told

That I know tomorrow
even if I haven't been there
we don't need amulets or
lucky charms of gold and silver

Riza Ramos

The future is untold
we have plans we have dreams
what we hoped and envisioned
may not be all as it seems

I dance work and play
I love hard and singing loud
happy and worry-free
unafraid of what tomorrow brings me

That I know tomorrow
even if I haven't been there
what the Creator has designed
is for all of us to share

Home

Waking up in the morning
I smell the rice fields
brown leaves golden grains
years of good yields

Sipping hot tea in the afternoon
watching the coconut tree's
long green leaves swinging
some trunk filled with bees

Making beds in the evening
I hear the noise from the crickets
forming a band of tambourines
nightly concert with no tickets

I smell the roses at dawn
blossoming reds whites and yellows
long stems I forgot to trim
are crawling by my windows

Listening to my favorite music at noon
somebody knocks at my front door
a delivery man with gifts and flowers
I am the happiest of all mothers

Riza Ramos

Glimpse of Saipan

Listening to the waves
watching the sunset
dipping my toes
into the salty warm seawater
the small pack of gray fish
rushed to get home
before it gets dark
the smoke from the grill
of island barbecue flavor
waving friends in the street
unplanned dinner date
the man with the plate
chewing betel nut
chewing cigarettes
red stains on the patio
red stains on the streets
Oh I love all of it

Under the Marianas Moon

She had walked along Beach Road one late
        afternoon,
Upon the blue Marianas waters shone the
        translucent moon,
The scene hasn't changed much:
        the wharf, the bench, the trees
and neither the winds across the Philippine Sea

As she sat on the bench, Norfolk Pines
        touched the sky,
The tide seemed stronger than in the evenings
        gone by,
He approached with the breeze and as much
        as the same pace
and both lifted their spirits as she lifted her face

His smile, she recalls, sparkled with twinkling grace
That smile hasn't changed since she first saw his
        face
In his eyes were magic-like stars shooting through
        the sky
Broad shoulders, strong physique, deep long sigh
He uttered no words but his loneliness peaked
        through
Her eyes, too, spoke of pain forever connecting
        the two

The evening was silent as they sat side by side
Just the moon up above, and the breeze, and the tide

Just a glimpse of him in Garapan Street
        is a moment to be glad
Though she still bore the pain of the thoughts
        she once had
Looking back through the years when they were
        islands apart
Nothing ever lessened the flame from that
        auspicious start

Tomorrow that moon will seem like a world far
        away
She'll remember Beach Road and that one
        fateful day
In that same open space where they forgave,
        and will forget
A new dream and a new start as they watch the
        sunset

One more glimpse at the skies, and the moon
        seems bolder
The tide is getting closer, and the air seems
        much colder
Times have changed, but things will never be like
        that day
Love defies the odds and the curse of being away.

Let the children have some fun.
Let the children play under the sun.

There's an Island paradise
surrounded by oceans
with green lush mountains
I feast my eyes
a yellow kite
lovers parasailing in pairs
in crisp mid-noon sunlight
banana boats
friendly locals
sunset fades transformed into dark
tourist ready to embark on the yacht
the band starts to play
local songs and YMCA
oh I never get tired of it
every day that I went
to the beach —
Saipan

*Dusk comes again, that dusk cannot defeat
the man who wants to see the dawn.*

Dusk and Dawn

He saw the dusk masked the horizon
the day slowly concealed by darkness
he waited for the dawn
and for the sun to peak slowly at the east
three days the dusk and dawn his clock
aching body stretched on a cold rough rock
at night the crickets made some company
singing sweet songs to ease his agony
cracked lips dry mouth numb feet
he slowly closed his tired droopy eyes
dusk may come again
but dusk cannot defeat
the man who wants to see the dawn
daylight
Sugar King Park Saipan
Here's another wounded soldier
He's a veteran
He's strong
He survived

I Learned

that success is how we define it
I learned
that dreams and aspirations
aren't ours to meet
rather our guides
we're not here to decide
for the universe got some plans
of their own

I learned to be strong
when everyone else breaks
and when everyone brags
I learned to be humble and meek
I learned to walk away
but also fought back
I've learned
that friends can change colors
some weren't there
when I was down
but rather walked away with a frown
I learned to be patient
when everyone else rushed
I learned to wait for more
and choose whom to trust

Riza Ramos

I learned to discern
unreasonable senseless stuff
from what is essential
I learned that big or small
everyone else is special

Faith reveals the secrets of the universe.

Poems
About the
Secrets
of the Universe

Real Friends

Real friends emerge
in darkness and drought
you don't have to
say a single word
or help be sought

Riza Ramos

Some Path of Beans

I didn't intend to be here
like some path of beans
led me to this place
the map unfolded
our story was plotted
before we even met
that you and I will be here
in the place we least expected
I had no plans to be here
the oceans divided
made a path for me
to cross like Moses
the night was so dark
but the streetlights
lead me here in your arms

The Quilt

For years
I'd been haunted
by the perplexity
as to why things
happen the way they do
I'd been hit by
bunch of snags
undesirable
uncontrollable
circumstances seemingly
attracted to me
they're thieves
who struck me
unaware
they're sleeping giants
awaken and provoked
some tests
I embraced this belief
unwanted situations are tests
to my faith
and my endurance as a human

unfavorable things
happened by purpose
time has revealed every fiber of it
I stitched
every single inch of fabric
one by one
and created a masterpiece

After the Storm

I saw the rainbow
purple green and yellow
many colors of hope
such a magical hue

the wind gracefully stopped howling
the night slowly shifted to dawn
the sun started to smile

the waves and tides became still
small pieces of battered flowers and leaves
blown to our windowsill
birds started to sing
I thanked the heavens
for when the storm abated
he kept me and my loved ones safe

God Is There

In the coldest places
where the sun doesn't show
in the darkest places
where no trees will ever grow
in the driest deserts
where no flowers bloom
God is there
even
in the midst of the storm

Plea to the Moon and Sun

Glow lovely moon glow
unto my nights so dim
besides the stars and planets
shine bright to guide my dreams

Shine bright fierce sun
unto the road I'm taking
make my days brighter
to guide my undertakings

River

If I can change
the course of the river
I will let the water flow
to where I want it to go

but since I can't
I will trust the stream
and go with the flow

It's Not About Me

It's not about the game
it's how I play it
it's not about the music
it's how I dance to the tune
it's not about what I feel
but how I perceive other's feelings
it's not about words
it's how I process them
it's not all about what I see
but what is hidden
it's not about what I hear
but what is unspoken
it's not about what I have
but how I learn to live without
this isn't about me
neither about you
this is something about life

Breathe

Breathe
you're not a thing
you didn't come from nowhere
you're a human being
you have a heart
you have feelings
you are a perfect creation
a perfect mold
one to behold
you have a purpose
and everything else does
the bugs
the trees
the vines
the pines
the peas
the mountains
the birds
the paper
the flowers
the wise man's words
the roses' thorns

Success Is

Success is
always a work in progress
it never ceases
until you call it quits
success is a work of art
not with so much brain
but needs a steadfast heart
success sometimes is to finish what you start
success is something
we need not to ask when we pray
sometimes it's a balance between work and play
for life will be dull and tedious
with hardwork success is within grasp
success is just around the corner
in the mountains in the seas it's everywhere
so open all doors when it knocks
listen to the whispers of luck
success
there are no definite rules
it could be in the south
it could be in the north
or in any other roads

Making a Difference

I felt elated
when I got hold
of the things I waited
and the things I longed
for many years
I can't contain
the happiness within
as I picked the fruits
of my patience
I am the proudest
I harvested the crop
of my blood and sweat
I smiled
when I looked back and remembered
how they turned their backs on me
I believed in me
because I got no one to turn to
I shouted
let the whole world know
that I made a difference
even without you

Some Days I Think of This

Opportunity is not to be chased
when I'm the one to create
love is not to be begged
when I'm the one to give
kindness is not to be cherished
when I'm the one to embrace
the future is not to be feared
when I'm the one to lead

Not Everything

is given by God
most of these we have to work hard
He gave us the body
He gave us the brains
He gave us the wit
that you and me
will be free
of any decisions
we make

To Love

is to think about it
every time every minute
in the sink while doing the dishes
in the oven while baking cookies

to love is easy
it can develop over time
but to rekindle the love
from the heart that was shattered
from the heart that lost its trust
is threading a needle
by a poor eyesight

Riza Ramos

What's the Meaning of Life

Some people got everything they need
yet may be unhappy
I wonder why

Some people could barely eat
but know how to put
a smile on their faces
I wonder why

Some people made their dreams
and living it
yet may complain and whine
I wonder why

Some people try to make ends meet
day by day
but no sense of weary
I wonder why

What's the real meaning of life
I wonder what

What Are You

all of us play a role
a clown
a dancer
a lady
a beau
a confidante
a critique
a friend
a foe

Cultivate Love

Time will come
that money and wealth
will not be enough
so
I will cultivate and plant some love
much love than the water in the ocean
much love than the air in the stratosphere
I will sprinkle kindness
much kindness than the rain that feeds the forest
and will spread generosity
to where it is needed
some dark corners of the earth
I guees
the purest legacy
where no barometer of wealth
can measure
is not the weight of our gold
and someday
it's the love and kindness
we have given to be told

Turn

Envy
not the things
you don't own
that others may have

patience
hard work
you'll get what you need
the wheel turns

cry not
over spilled moments
setbacks
frustrations
you will gain
what you dreamt
life goes on
the wheel turns

Riza Ramos

Stump

It's been many years
she hasn't visited the place
where they first met

she wondered
if their names were still there
on the tree trunk they engraved
and the huge branch
that leaned to the ground
where they used to sit

she saw nothing but some stump
almost swallowed
by the thick long grass
and some red roses that crawled

I Know Tomorrow

Soft Stones

It's hard to linger on the past
the past that mostly hurts
but let's make use of our pains
to inspire us to move further —
to succeed
those who looked down on us
would look up instead
and those who broke our heart
will surely regret

looking back
if they didn't treat us right
we can prove them wrong
by making some soft bread
out of hard stones

Colors

life can be full of colors
you messed around
you played around
you made mistakes
learned the lessons
and made amends

you were so proud of what you'd been through
with no regrets and resentments
and decided to color your story with ink

Duck

A scoop of rice
and spicy scrambled eggs
high hair bun neatly sprayed
ironed scrubs tucked in
compression white stockings
distant hugs and kisses for my baby
be safe my dear mommy
I thanked God for each day
for making me strong and healthy
to fight this unseen enemy
another glass of warm water
another quick bathroom trip
protective white suit size petite
fitted N95 face mask and shield

I am a soldier without ammunition
just a heart full of compassion
a bladder with 3 liters capacity
iron feet buffalo knees

massive sweat all over me
that's how it ends the day
as I face the mirror
the N95 face mask left some mark
I saw a duck!

I Wonder

Sometimes I wonder
why God has not given what I prayed for
only to learn it wasn't good enough for me

sometimes I ponder
why God has kept me waiting for too long
only to learn that God wants something more

sometimes I ask
why God has kept me waiting much longer
only to learn that
God does not want something better
but something best

Inspire

There's no point in giving up
your dreams
when you realized
somebody out there wants
to be in your shoes
to be where you are right now
you might think
that what you got
is not enough
but the blessings overflow
and you must realize it's true

Don't say no
to someone who looks up to you
you don't know
how you inspired them
to see the things you've seen
to embrace the ambiance
of your place
to breathe the air you inhale
to be just like you

Continue to do what you do
gently embrace the life you have
for no one else can carry on like you
No one
don't quit listening to the birds
Be sensitive

Don't ignore the signs of the universe
they're everywhere
when you applied for a job
clad in your dainty formal garment
while on your way
the rain has stopped
If you doubted yourself
people who believe in you
will hesitate
inspire
though deep inside you cry

inspired by my former Nurse Manager Karlo R.

Mother Nature

Amid the heavy rain,
floods and storms.
Amid the hurricanes,
landslides or typhoons.
You asked, "Where's the sun?"
Centuries have passed that mankind
has abused nature —
cutting trees,
mining,
tons of trashes thrown.
Nature's wrath is unkind.
"It's payback time!" Mother Nature said.
Humans, are you not scared?

A Wish

I can only wish
a world free of chaos
air free of pollution
humans free of disease
Mother Earth to be free of calamities
like storms, hurricanes and earthquakes

I cannot change the world
but I can write a poem

Thank You Poetry

Thank you poetry
you are there when I am lonely
sewing words daintily
rhyming them neatly

Thank you poetry
you are there when I am happy
putting those thoughts into words hastily
when emotions burst freely

Thank you poetry
you are there when no one else would
when no one else seems to listen
when no one else seems to care

Riza Ramos

Tomorrow

There are many things I'm quite certain
about tomorrow
the sun will still rise
the rivers will still flow
the wind will still blow
the sky will not fall

we will continue to dream
we will continue to love
life goes on
I'm wearing my scrubs

and tomorrow
we will forgive
what caused
our hearts bled.

www.ingramcontent.com/pod-product-compliance
Lightning Source LLC
LaVergne TN
LVHW021516080426
835509LV00018B/2538